Watch Out!

by Elizabeth Moore

Consultant:
Adria F. Klein, Ph.D.
California State University, San Bernardino

capstone
classroom

Heinemann Raintree • Red Brick Learning
division of Capstone

Stop on red.

Go on green.

Slow down on yellow.

Watch out when you ride.

Watch out when you drive.

Watch out when you walk.

Watch out when you play.